Thank you for being our valued customer

We will be grateful if you shared this happy experience in the online review section.
This helps us to continue providing great products
and helps potential buyers to make a confident decision.

check my booklets collection on amazon under this name
AUTHOR NAME: *DogVaccination Publishing Record*

Brand Name: Zebra Lines Publishing

PHOTO OF ME AND MY PET

THIS BOOK BELONGS TO

NAME :

ADDRESS :

PHONE :

PET OWNER DETAILS

NAME :

SURNAME :

ADDRESS :

POSTCODE :

CITY :

PHONE NUMBER :

EMAIL :

NOTES :

PET DETAILS

NAME :

BREED :

BIRTHDAY :

GENDER :

ID CHIP :

ALLERGIES :

SKIN COLOR:

EYE COLOR:

WEIGHT:

MEDICAL CONDITIONS:

SPECIAL MARKINGS:

VET. INFO

NAME :

PHONE :

EMAIL :

ADDRESS :

HOSPITAL INFO

NAME/BUSINESS :

PHONE :

EMAIL :

ADDRESS :

PET INSURANCE DETAILS

INSURANCE COMPANY:

POLICY TYPE:

POLICY NUMBER:

CONTACT:

DETAILS:

 # VACCINATION LOG BOOK

DATE	AGE	WEIGHT	VACCINE	BRAND	BATCH#	VET.

NOTES : _____
_____
_____

MY PET
DAILY CARE
CHECKLIST

DATE	FOOD	WATER	WALK	BATH

VET. VISIT LOG

DATE : _____

AGE : _____ TIME : _____

Routine Visit : ____ Emergency Visit : ____

VET. DETAILS : _____

REASON FOR VISIT : _____

SHOTS : _____

MEDICATION : _____

OTHER TREATMENT : _____

COMMENTS : _____

NOTES :

VACCINATION LOG BOOK

DATE	AGE	WEIGHT	VACCINE	BRAND	BATCH#	VET.

NOTES :

_____

....

....

....

....

....

....

....

....

....

....

....

....

....

....

....

STAMPS PAGE

VACCINATION LOG BOOK

DATE	AGE	WEIGHT	VACCINE	BRAND	BATCH#	VET.

NOTES : _____
_____
_____

MY PET
DAILY CARE
CHECKLIST

DATE	FOOD	WATER	WALK	BATH

VET. VISIT LOG

DATE : ....

AGE : ( )   **TIME :** ( )

Routine Visit : ( )   **Emergency Visit :** ( )

VET. DETAILS : ( )

( )

REASON FOR VISIT : ( )

SHOTS : ( )

MEDICATION : ( )

OTHER TREATMENT : ( )

COMMENTS : ( )

NOTES :

_____

_____

_____

_____

VACCINATION LOG BOOK

DATE	AGE	WEIGHT	VACCINE	BRAND	BATCH#	VET.

NOTES :

VET. VISIT NOTES

 # VACCINATION LOG BOOK

DATE	AGE	WEIGHT	VACCINE	BRAND	BATCH#	VET.

NOTES : _____

_____

_____

MY PET
DAILY CARE
CHECKLIST

DATE	FOOD	WATER	WALK	BATH

 **VET. VISIT LOG**

DATE : ....

AGE : ⬭   TIME : ⬭

Routine Visit : ⬭   Emergency Visit : ⬭

VET. DETAILS :

REASON FOR VISIT :

SHOTS :

MEDICATION :

OTHER TREATMENT :

COMMENTS :

NOTES :

VACCINATION LOG BOOK

DATE	AGE	WEIGHT	VACCINE	BRAND	BATCH#	VET.

NOTES : _____
_____
_____

VET. VISIT NOTES

STAMPS PAGE

STAMPS PAGE

VACCINATION LOG BOOK

DATE	AGE	WEIGHT	VACCINE	BRAND	BATCH#	VET.

NOTES :

 VACCINATION LOG BOOK

DATE	AGE	WEIGHT	VACCINE	BRAND	BATCH#	VET.

NOTES : _____

_____

_____

MY PET
DAILY CARE
CHECKLIST

DATE	FOOD	WATER	WALK	BATH

# VET. VISIT LOG

DATE : ....

AGE : ⬭ TIME : ⬭

Routine Visit : ⬭ Emergency Visit : ⬭

VET. DETAILS : ⬭

⬭

REASON FOR VISIT : ⬭

SHOTS : ⬭

MEDICATION : ⬭

OTHER TREATMENT : ⬭

COMMENTS : ⬭

NOTES :

VACCINATION LOG BOOK

DATE	AGE	WEIGHT	VACCINE	BRAND	BATCH#	VET.

NOTES : _____

_____

_____

STAMPS PAGE

VACCINATION LOG BOOK

DATE	AGE	WEIGHT	VACCINE	BRAND	BATCH#	VET.

NOTES : _____

_____

_____

MY PET
DAILY CARE
CHECKLIST

DATE	FOOD	WATER	WALK	BATH

VET. VISIT LOG

DATE : ....

AGE : ⬭ TIME : ⬭

Routine Visit : ⬭ Emergency Visit : ⬭

VET. DETAILS : ⬭

⬭

REASON FOR VISIT : ⬭

SHOTS : ⬭

MEDICATION : ⬭

OTHER TREATMENT : ⬭

COMMENTS : ⬭

NOTES :

VACCINATION LOG BOOK

DATE	AGE	WEIGHT	VACCINE	BRAND	BATCH#	VET.

NOTES : _____

_____

_____

VET. VISIT NOTES

STAMPS PAGE

 # VACCINATION LOG BOOK

DATE	AGE	WEIGHT	VACCINE	BRAND	BATCH#	VET.

NOTES : _____
_____
_____

MY PET
DAILY CARE
CHECKLIST

DATE	FOOD	WATER	WALK	BATH

VET. VISIT LOG

DATE :

AGE : **TIME :**

Routine Visit : **Emergency Visit :**

VET. DETAILS :

REASON FOR VISIT :

SHOTS :

MEDICATION :

OTHER TREATMENT :

COMMENTS :

NOTES :

VACCINATION LOG BOOK

DATE	AGE	WEIGHT	VACCINE	BRAND	BATCH#	VET.

NOTES : _____

_____

_____

VET. VISIT NOTES

_____

# STAMPS PAGE

VACCINATION LOG BOOK

DATE	AGE	WEIGHT	VACCINE	BRAND	BATCH#	VET.

NOTES :

MY PET
DAILY CARE
CHECKLIST

DATE	FOOD	WATER	WALK	BATH

VET. VISIT LOG

DATE : ....

AGE : ⬡ **TIME :** ⬡

Routine Visit : ⬡ **Emergency Visit :** ⬡

VET. DETAILS :

REASON FOR VISIT :

SHOTS :

MEDICATION :

OTHER TREATMENT :

COMMENTS :

NOTES :

 # VACCINATION LOG BOOK

DATE	AGE	WEIGHT	VACCINE	BRAND	BATCH#	VET.

NOTES : _____
_____
_____

VET. VISIT NOTES

_____

....

....

....

....

....

....

....

....

....

....

....

....

....

....

....

....

....

# STAMPS PAGE

 **VACCINATION LOG BOOK**

DATE	AGE	WEIGHT	VACCINE	BRAND	BATCH#	VET.

NOTES : _____
_____
_____

MY PET
DAILY CARE
CHECKLIST

DATE	FOOD	WATER	WALK	BATH

VET. VISIT LOG

DATE : _____

AGE : ⬭ **TIME :** ⬭

Routine Visit : ⬭ **Emergency Visit :** ⬭

VET. DETAILS : _____

_____

REASON FOR VISIT : _____

SHOTS : _____

MEDICATION : _____

OTHER TREATMENT : _____

COMMENTS : _____

NOTES :

_____

_____

_____

_____

 # VACCINATION LOG BOOK

DATE	AGE	WEIGHT	VACCINE	BRAND	BATCH#	VET.

NOTES : _____
_____
_____

VET. VISIT NOTES

STAMPS PAGE

VACCINATION LOG BOOK

DATE	AGE	WEIGHT	VACCINE	BRAND	BATCH#	VET.

NOTES : _____

_____

_____

MY PET
DAILY CARE
CHECKLIST

DATE	FOOD	WATER	WALK	BATH

VET. VISIT LOG

DATE : ....

AGE : ( ) **TIME :** ( )

Routine Visit : ( ) **Emergency Visit :** ( )

VET. DETAILS : ( )
( )

REASON FOR VISIT : ( )

SHOTS : ( )

MEDICATION : ( )

OTHER TREATMENT : ( )

COMMENTS : ( )

NOTES :

 # VACCINATION LOG BOOK

DATE	AGE	WEIGHT	VACCINE	BRAND	BATCH#	VET.

NOTES :

_____

STAMPS PAGE

 VACCINATION LOG BOOK

DATE	AGE	WEIGHT	VACCINE	BRAND	BATCH#	VET.

NOTES :

MY PET
DAILY CARE
CHECKLIST

DATE	FOOD	WATER	WALK	BATH

VET. VISIT LOG

DATE : ....

AGE : ( )   TIME : ( )

Routine Visit : ( )   Emergency Visit : ( )

VET. DETAILS : ( )

( )

REASON FOR VISIT : ( )

SHOTS : ( )

MEDICATION : ( )

OTHER TREATMENT : ( )

COMMENTS : ( )

NOTES :

_____

_____

_____

_____

 # VACCINATION LOG BOOK

DATE	AGE	WEIGHT	VACCINE	BRAND	BATCH#	VET.

NOTES : _____
_____
_____

VET. VISIT NOTES

STAMPS PAGE

 **VACCINATION LOG BOOK**

DATE	AGE	WEIGHT	VACCINE	BRAND	BATCH#	VET.

NOTES : _____

_____

_____

MY PET
DAILY CARE
CHECKLIST

DATE	FOOD	WATER	WALK	BATH

VET. VISIT LOG

DATE : ....

AGE : ⬭ TIME : ⬭

Routine Visit : ⬭ Emergency Visit : ⬭

VET. DETAILS : ⬭

⬭

REASON FOR VISIT : ⬭

SHOTS : ⬭

MEDICATION : ⬭

OTHER TREATMENT : ⬭

COMMENTS : ⬭

NOTES :

 # VACCINATION LOG BOOK

DATE	AGE	WEIGHT	VACCINE	BRAND	BATCH#	VET.

NOTES :

VACCINATION LOG BOOK

DATE	AGE	WEIGHT	VACCINE	BRAND	BATCH#	VET.

NOTES : _____

_____

_____

MY PET
DAILY CARE
CHECKLIST

DATE	FOOD	WATER	WALK	BATH

VET. VISIT LOG

DATE : ....

AGE : _____   **TIME :** _____

Routine Visit : ___   **Emergency Visit :** ___

VET. DETAILS : _____
_____

REASON FOR VISIT : _____

SHOTS : _____

MEDICATION : _____

OTHER TREATMENT : _____

COMMENTS : _____

NOTES :
_____
_____
_____
_____

VACCINATION LOG BOOK

DATE	AGE	WEIGHT	VACCINE	BRAND	BATCH#	VET.

NOTES : _____
_____
_____

VET. VISIT NOTES

_____

STAMPS PAGE

 **VACCINATION LOG BOOK**

DATE	AGE	WEIGHT	VACCINE	BRAND	BATCH#	VET.

NOTES :

MY PET
DAILY CARE
CHECKLIST

DATE	FOOD	WATER	WALK	BATH

VET. VISIT LOG

DATE : _____

AGE : _____ TIME : _____

Routine Visit : __ Emergency Visit : __

VET. DETAILS : _____

_____

REASON FOR VISIT : _____

SHOTS : _____

MEDICATION : _____

OTHER TREATMENT : _____

COMMENTS : _____

NOTES :
_____
_____
_____
_____

VACCINATION LOG BOOK

DATE	AGE	WEIGHT	VACCINE	BRAND	BATCH#	VET.

NOTES : _____

_____

_____

VACCINATION LOG BOOK

DATE	AGE	WEIGHT	VACCINE	BRAND	BATCH#	VET.

NOTES : _____

_____

_____

MY PET
DAILY CARE
CHECKLIST

DATE	FOOD	WATER	WALK	BATH

VET. VISIT LOG

DATE : ....

AGE : ⬭ TIME : ⬭

Routine Visit : ⬭ **Emergency Visit :** ⬭

VET. DETAILS : ⬭

⬭

REASON FOR VISIT : ⬭

SHOTS : ⬭

MEDICATION : ⬭

OTHER TREATMENT : ⬭

COMMENTS : ⬭

NOTES :

_____

_____

_____

_____

VACCINATION LOG BOOK

DATE	AGE	WEIGHT	VACCINE	BRAND	BATCH#	VET.

NOTES : _____
_____
_____

VET. VISIT NOTES

STAMPS PAGE

VACCINATION LOG BOOK

DATE	AGE	WEIGHT	VACCINE	BRAND	BATCH#	VET.

NOTES :

MY PET
DAILY CARE
CHECKLIST

DATE	FOOD	WATER	WALK	BATH

VET. VISIT LOG

DATE : ....

AGE : ( )   TIME : ( )

Routine Visit : ( )   Emergency Visit : ( )

VET. DETAILS : ( )

( )

REASON FOR VISIT : ( )

SHOTS : ( )

MEDICATION : ( )

OTHER TREATMENT : ( )

COMMENTS : ( )

NOTES :

VACCINATION LOG BOOK

DATE	AGE	WEIGHT	VACCINE	BRAND	BATCH#	VET.

NOTES : _____

_____

_____

✿✿✿ VACCINATION LOG BOOK ✿✿✿

DATE	AGE	WEIGHT	VACCINE	BRAND	BATCH#	VET.

NOTES : _____
_____
_____

VACCINATION LOG BOOK

DATE	AGE	WEIGHT	VACCINE	BRAND	BATCH#	VET.

NOTES :

Made in United States
Troutdale, OR
10/08/2024

23561114R00062